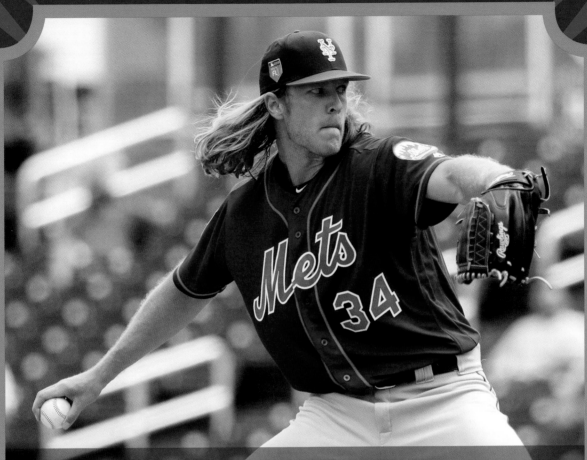

NEW YORK
METS
STARS, STATS, HISTORY, AND MORE!

BY K. C. KELLEY

Published by The Child's World®
1980 Lookout Drive • Mankato, MN 56003-1705
800-599-READ • www.childsworld.com

ISBN 9781503828315
LCCN 2018944845

Printed in the United States of America
PAO2392

Photo Credits:
Cover: Joe Robbins (2).
Inside: AP Images: 8, Bill Kostroun 11, 17, Kathy Willens 19;
Dreamstime.com: Anthony Aneese Totah Jr. 12, Alan Tan
Photography 14, Jerry Coli 23; Newscom: Ron Sachs/
PictureAlliance 7, Rich Graessle/Icon SMI 20, Rich von
Bilberstein/Icon SW 27; Joe Robbins 4, 24, 29.

About the Author

K.C. Kelley is a huge sports
fan who has written more
than 100 books for kids. His
favorite sport is baseball.
He has also written about
football, basketball, soccer,
and even auto racing! He lives
in Santa Barbara, California.

On the Cover

Main photo: Mets ace
Noah Syndergaard
Inset: Hall of Famer Tom Seaver

CONTENTS

GO, METS!

New York City is big enough for two Major League Baseball (MLB) teams. The newest of the two is the Mets. The other team, the Yankees, is much more famous. Mets fans don't care, though. They love their hard-working **underdogs**! As the team's song goes, "Meet the Mets! Meet the Mets! C'mon, everybody, let's greet the Mets!"

◄ *Yoenis Cespedes gets high fives after hitting another homer for the Mets!*

WHO ARE THE METS?

The Mets play in the National League (NL). That group is part of Major League Baseball (MLB). MLB also includes the American League (AL). There are 30 teams in MLB. The winner of the NL plays the winner of the AL in the **World Series**. Mets fans are devoted to their team. They have gone a long time without a championship. They're still cheering for one, though!

Jacob DeGrom has become one of the NL's top pitchers.

WHERE THEY CAME FROM

The Mets started in 1962. They were an **expansion** team as MLB grew larger. The team's name is short for "Metropolitan." That's a fancy word for a big city. The Mets play in a part of New York City called Queens. It is on Long Island, so many Mets fans live there, to the east of the team's stadium. The Mets started slowly, but have had several great seasons since then.

◄ *Jerry Grote played for the Mets for 12 seasons and helped them win a World Series.*

WHO THEY PLAY

The Mets play in the NL East Division. The other teams in the NL East are the Atlanta Braves, the Miami Marlins, the Philadelphia Phillies, and the Washington Nationals. The Mets play more games against their division **rivals** than against other teams. In all, the Mets play 162 games each season. They play 81 games at home and 81 on the road. When the Mets play the Yankees, the games are called the Subway Series. Fans get to the games on the underground trains!

He's out! Asdrubal Cabrera has just tagged ➤
out a player on the Mets' rival, the Yankees.

WHERE THEY PLAY

CitiField is a gem of a ballpark. It opened in 2009. The stadium uses lots of brick. It has an old-time feeling. To remember a baseball great, CitiField has a statue of Jackie Robinson. He played for the Brooklyn Dodgers. He was the first African American MLB player in the 20th century. The Mets wanted to honor him! In front of the ballpark, a huge apple rises out of a top hat. New York City's nickname is "The Big Apple."

 Fans line up to get inside CitiField and cheer on the Mets.

THE BASEBALL FIELD

OUTFIELD

◄ FOUL LINE

THIRD BASE ▼

COACH'S BOX ➤

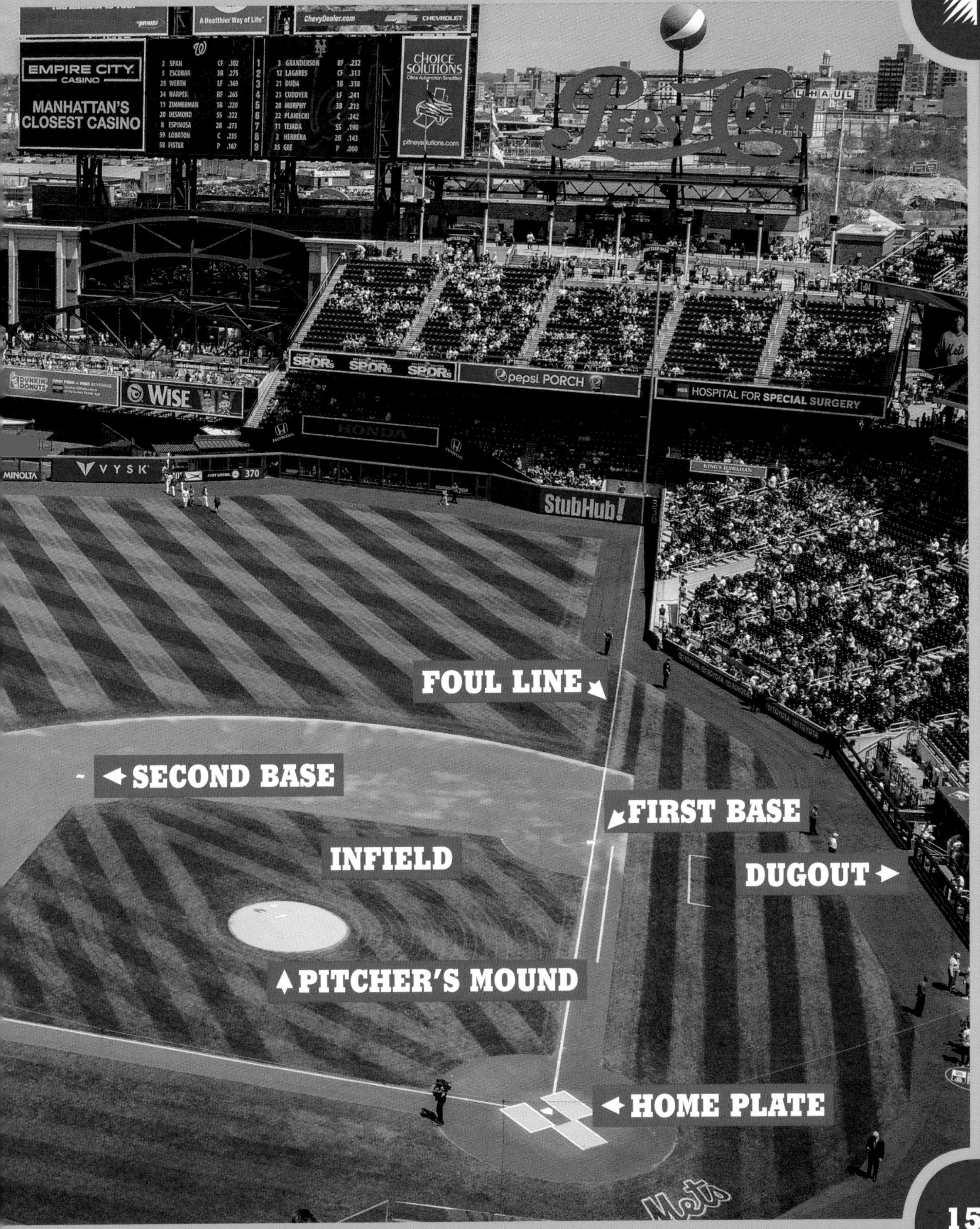

FOUL LINE
SECOND BASE
FIRST BASE
INFIELD
DUGOUT
PITCHER'S MOUND
HOME PLATE
EMPIRE CITY CASINO
MANHATTAN'S CLOSEST CASINO
CHOICE SOLUTIONS
PEPSI-COLA
pepsi PORCH
HOSPITAL FOR SPECIAL SURGERY
WISE
StubHub!
HONDA
Mets

BIG DAYS

The Mets have had a lot of great days in their long history. Here are a few of them.

1969—The "Miracle Mets" won their first and only World Series. They were way behind in August but **rallied**. The champs were led by pitcher Tom Seaver, a future Hall of Famer.

2000—This was the biggest Subway Series ever. The Mets played the Yankees in the World Series. All the games were in New York City for the first time since 1956. The Mets lost the Series, but it was a great ride for fans.

Happy Mets fans poured onto the field after the ➤ Mets won the 1969 World Series.

2015—The Mets won the NL championship. It was their first since 2000. The team had some of the best pitchers in the league. Second baseman Daniel Murphy was a top **slugger**. New York lost the World Series to the Kansas City Royals. Still, it was a great season.

TOUGH DAYS

Like every team, the Mets have had some not-so-great days, too. Here are a few their fans might not want to recall.

1973—Four years after they won the World Series, the Mets earned another trip to the championship. Sadly, the Mets couldn't win the final two games to the Oakland A's and lost the Series.

1977—Mets fans were very sad when the team traded ace Tom Seaver to the Cincinnati Reds. Called "Tom Terrific," he was one of the best Mets players ever.

A Phillies player runs home after hitting a homer in ➤ *2007. Mets pitcher Jorge Sosa can only watch.*

2007—The Mets were ahead by seven games with just 17 left in the season. They had the NL East in the bag! And then they didn't. They lost six of their last seven games. The final loss was 8-1 to the lowly Phillies. The Mets did *not* win the NL East!

MEET THE FANS!

Mets fans love their team! In baseball-crazy New York City, though, they sometimes feel like second place. That makes Mets fans more loyal than ever! The fans fill CitiField and cheer for every pitch. They have some help. One of baseball's most famous mascots is the baseball-headed Mr. Met!

◀ *Seeing Mr. Met's giant baseball head means it's time for Mets baseball!*

HEROES THEN

The "Miracle Mets" of 1969 had some great players. Pitcher Tom Seaver had one of baseball's best fastballs. He led the NL in strikeouts five times with the Mets. In 1986, the Mets were led by slugger Darryl Strawberry and pitching **ace** Dwight "Doc" Gooden. Later, Mike Piazza was one of the best hitting catchers ever. Third baseman David Wright was among the all-time leaders in hitting for the Mets.

Seaver threw so hard his right leg always scraped ➤
the dirt. See the dusty patch on his uniform!

HEROES NOW

Thor! That's what fans called pitcher Noah Syndegaard. He throws lightning bolts and has long hair like the comic book hero. Jacob DeGrom is another top pitcher. He set an MLB record in 2018. He gave up three runs or fewer in 26 straight starts! Outfielder Yoenis Cespedes is the team's top home run hitter.

◄ Syndegaard usually strikes out at least one batter every inning.

GEARING UP

Baseball players wear team uniforms. On defense, they wear leather gloves to catch the ball. As batters, they wear hard helmets. This protects them from pitches. Batters hit the ball with long wood bats. Each player chooses his own size of bat. Catchers have the toughest job. They wear a lot of protection.

THE BASEBALL

The outside of the Major League baseball is made from cow leather. Two leather pieces shaped like 8's are stitched together. There are 108 stitches of red thread. These stitches help players grip the ball. Inside, the ball has a small center of cork and rubber. Hundreds of feet of yarn are tightly wound around this center.

CATCHER'S MASK AND HELMET

CHEST PROTECTOR

WRIST BAND

CATCHER'S MITT

SHIN GUARDS

CATCHER'S GEAR

TEAM STATS

Here are some of the all-time career records for the New York Mets. All of these stats are through the 2018 regular season.

BATTING AVERAGE

John Olerud	.315
Keith Hernandez	.297

RBI

David Wright	970
Darryl Strawberry	733

STOLEN BASES

Jose Reyes	406
Mookie Wilson	281

SAVES

John Franco	276
Armando Benitez	160

WINS

Tom Seaver	198
Dwight Gooden	157

STRIKEOUTS

Tom Seaver	2,541
Dwight Gooden	1,875

Wright was a seven-time All-Star for the Mets. ➤

HOME RUNS	
Darryl Strawberry	252
David Wright	242

GLOSSARY

ace (AYS) a team's top pitcher

expansion (ex-PAN-shun) when something gets larger

rallied (RAHL-eed) came from behind to win

rivals (RYE-vuhls) two people or groups competing for the same thing

slugger (SLUG-er) a hitter who hits a lot of home runs and extra-base hits

underdogs (UN-der-dogz) teams or athletes who are not expected to win

World Series (WURLD SEER-eez) the championship of Major League Baseball, played between the winners of the AL and NL

FIND OUT MORE

IN THE LIBRARY

Connery-Boyd, Peg. *New York Mets: Big Book of Activities*. Chicago, IL: Sourcebooks Jabberwocky, 2016.

Kelly, David. *Subway Series Surprise (Ballpark Mysteries)*. New York, NY: Random House Book for Young Readers, 2018.

Rhodes, Sam. *The New York Mets (Inside MLB)*. Calgary, AB: Weigl Publishers, 2018.

ON THE WEB

Visit our website for links about the New York Mets:
childsworld.com/links

Note to Parents, Teachers, and Librarians: We routinely verify our web links to make sure they are safe and active sites. So encourage your readers to check them out!

INDEX